S0-AFR-512

Was Your Stuff MADE Like It's MEDIEVAL Times?

Manufacturing Technology THEN and NOW

by Megan Cooley Peterson

Content Consultant:
James Masschaele, PhD
Professor of History, Executive Vice Dean
School of Arts and Sciences
Rutgers University

CAPSTONE PRESS
a capstone imprint

Captivate is published by Capstone Press, an imprint of Capstone.
1710 Roe Crest Drive
North Mankato, Minnesota 56003
www.capstonepub.com

Library of Congress Cataloging-in-Publication Data is available on the Library of Congress website.
ISBN: 978-1-4966-8470-7 (hardcover)
ISBN: 978-1-4966-8490-5 (eBook PDF)

Summary:
From windmills to wheelbarrows, medieval innovators helped develop or improve some important manufacturing technology we use today. The Middle Ages were crucial for the improvement of the spinning wheel, loom, printing press, and more! Discover how our stuff was made like it's the medieval times.

Image Credits
Alamy: Africa Media Online, 34, North Wind Picture Archives, Cover (Bottom Left), 43; Getty Images: Universal History Archive, 31; Granger: DeA Picture Library, 32; Mary Evans Picture Library: INTERPHOTO/D.H. Teuffen, 39; Newscom: AiWire, 21, 28-29, Oronoz/Album, 10, picture-alliance/dpa/Daniel Karmann, 40, Pictures From History, 24, Prisma/Album, 6, World History Archive, 25, 37; North Wind Picture Archives, 23; Shutterstock: alterfalter, Cover (Bottom Right), Ivan Yang, 16, Matyas Rehak, 12, Max4e Photo, 13, Opapa, 9, PhotoFires, 14, QiuJu Song, 27, SGr, 30, takabisha, 4, UfaBizPhoto, 19

Design Elements
Capstone; Shutterstock: andromina, Curly Pat, derGriza, Evgeniya Mokeeva, Kompaniets Taras, lightmood, ONYXprj, Tartila, yalcinart

Editorial Credits
Editor: Michelle Parkin; Designer: Sarah Bennett; Media Researcher: Jo Miller; Production Specialist: Katy LaVigne

Printed and bound in the United States of America.
PA117

Table of Contents

Words in **bold** are in the glossary.

CHAPTER 1

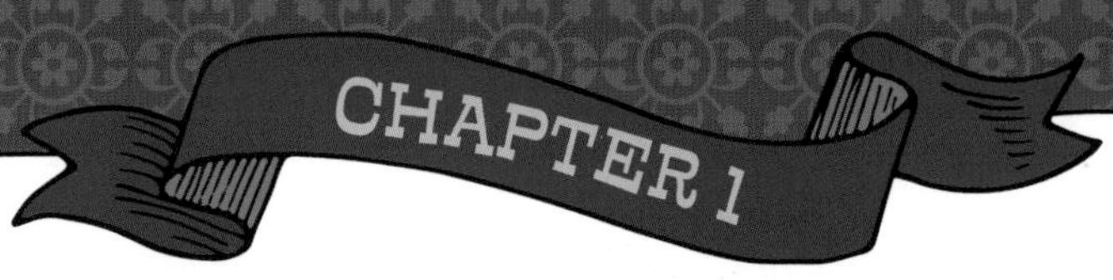

Manufacturing in a New Age

Imagine you're driving down the highway with your family. You sit in the backseat, reading your favorite book. Outside your window, hundreds of wind **turbines** spin, creating power. You get a chill and slip on the new jacket you bought at the mall.

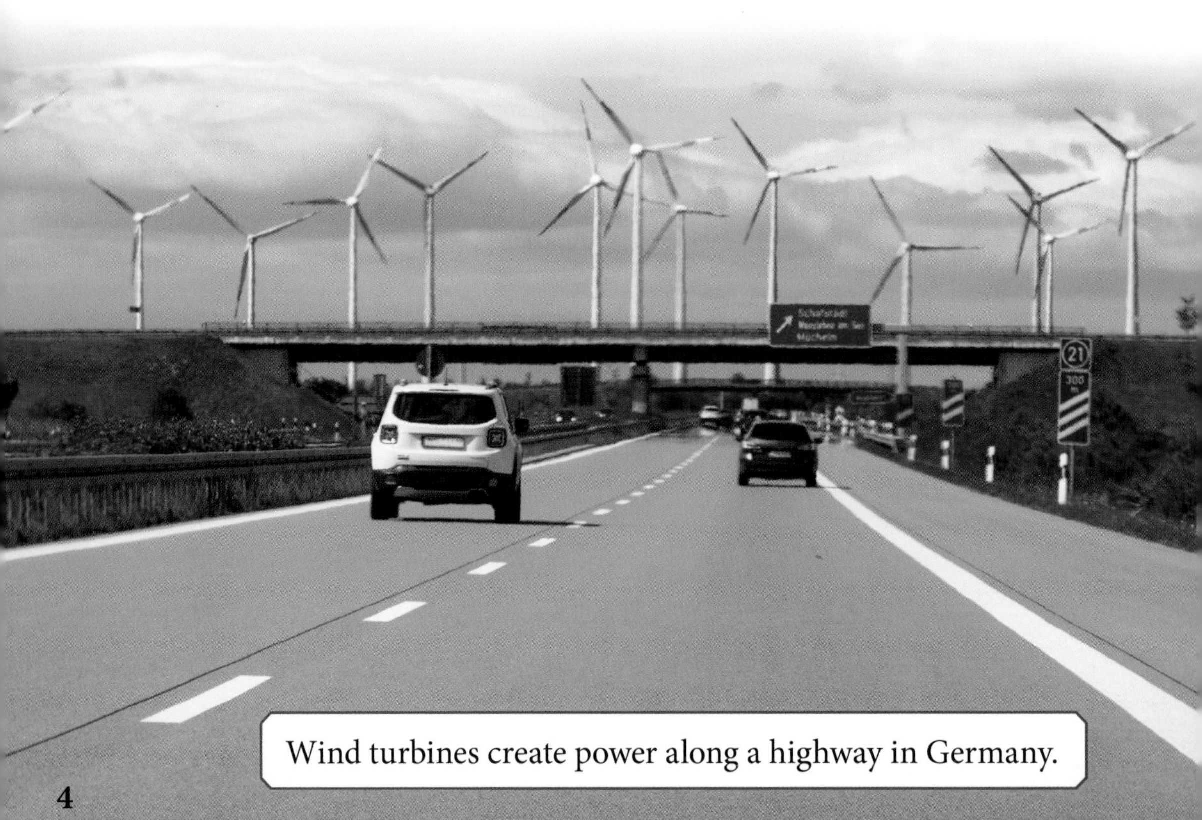

Wind turbines create power along a highway in Germany.

Now try to imagine life without wind power, printed books, and clothing that you can buy from a store. From the printing press to the windmill, the people of the Middle Ages developed **manufacturing** technology that we use every day.

The Middle Ages began around AD 476. The era lasted until about AD 1500. This time is divided into three ages: Early Middle Ages, High Middle Ages, and Late Middle Ages. The Middle Ages is often called medieval times.

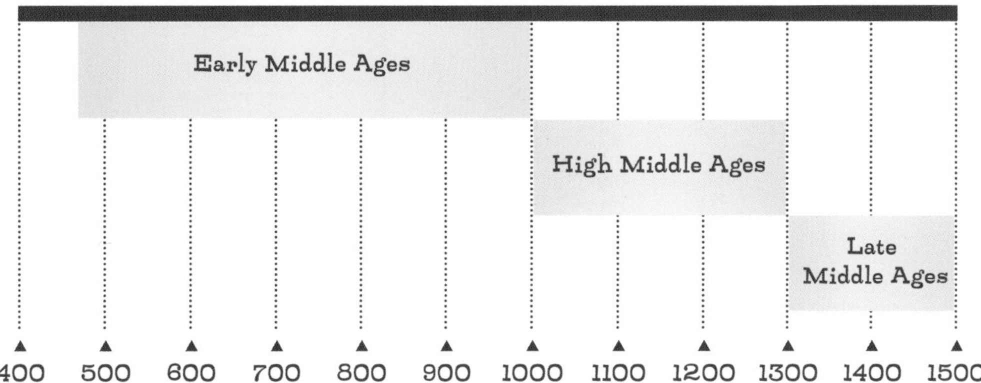

Medieval Life

Life during the Middle Ages wasn't easy. Medieval people didn't have the things we have today, such as running water and electricity. They had to make their own clothing and grow their own food. They needed to find ways to do more work while spending less physical energy. Workers invented new manufacturing technologies and improved upon existing ones.

In the Early Middle Ages, there wasn't much manufacturing. Medieval people did their best with the resources they had. But as the Middle Ages went on, they came up with new technologies to make their lives easier.

Medieval people harvested barley and wheat. They also grew fruits and vegetables.

The Heavy Plow

In 2010, farmers from around the world gathered in Manitoba, Canada. Volunteers at the Manitoba Agricultural Museum were hoping to set a world record. They had built the world's largest agricultural plow. Now they needed to pass one final test—use the plow to turn some dirt.

The world had never seen a plow like this. It was 77 feet (23 meters) wide. It had 66 plow bottoms. Each bottom would plow one row of dirt. Five 100-year-old tractors were hooked up to the plow. They started their engines and pulled the plow down the field. It worked! The new record had been set for the largest working plow in the world.

During the Middle Ages, most people worked as farmers or had jobs related to farming. They didn't have motorized equipment to plow, plant, and harvest their fields like farmers do today. Medieval farmers spent most of their days outside, working the land using only their own strength. They needed to find ways to grow more crops without using more of their own energy.

Today, powerful plows turn the soil for farming.

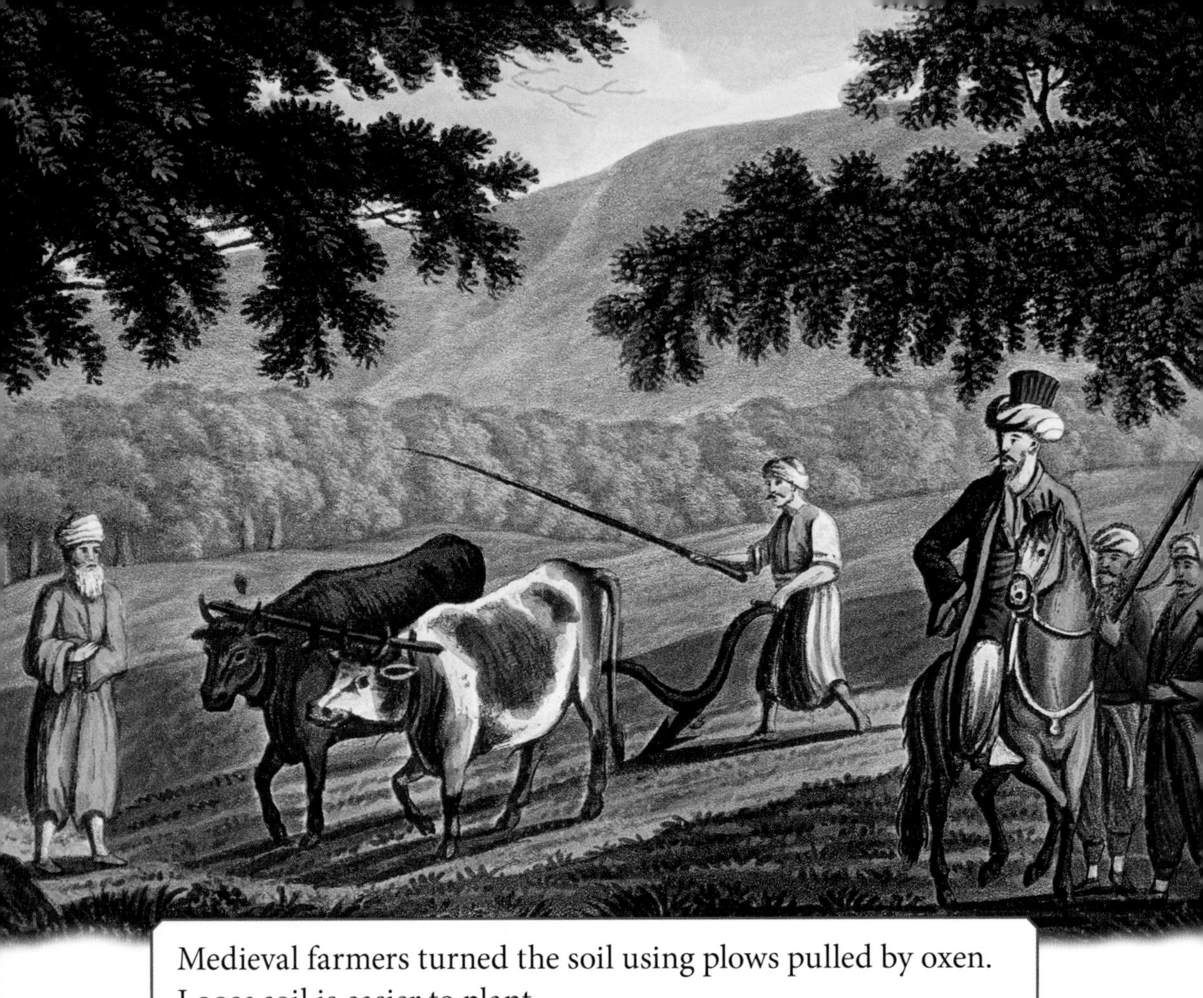

Medieval farmers turned the soil using plows pulled by oxen. Loose soil is easier to plant.

Before the Middle Ages, farmers used a simple plow called an ard, or scratch-plow. The scratch-plow had a sharp stick attached to a frame, which was pulled by oxen. The stick easily cut through the soil, but it couldn't turn the soil over. Farmers had to plow their fields twice—first one way and then again in the opposite direction.

Starting somewhere around AD 1000, farmers in Europe began using the heavy plow. Made of wood and iron, the heavy plow had three working parts. The coulter was a heavy knifelike tool made of iron. It cut vertically into the soil. The share cut through dirt horizontally. Finally, the mouldboard turned the dirt to the left or the right. The heavy plow saved time and energy.

Agriculture and Manufacturing

The heavy plow changed manufacturing during the Middle Ages. Farmers could grow more crops. This meant there was more grain that needed to be ground into flour. Medieval manufacturers developed water mills and windmills to grind grain. Without the heavy plow, some historians believe other medieval technology may not have advanced as quickly as it did.

CHAPTER 3

The Vertical Windmill

Thousands of wind turbines spin in China's Gobi Desert. The Gansu wind farm uses these wind turbines to make electricity. As the wind blows, the blades spin a **generator**. The spinning generator creates electricity. Power lines carry the electricity to homes and businesses.

The Gansu wind farm has more than 7,000 wind turbines. It is one of the world's largest wind farms.

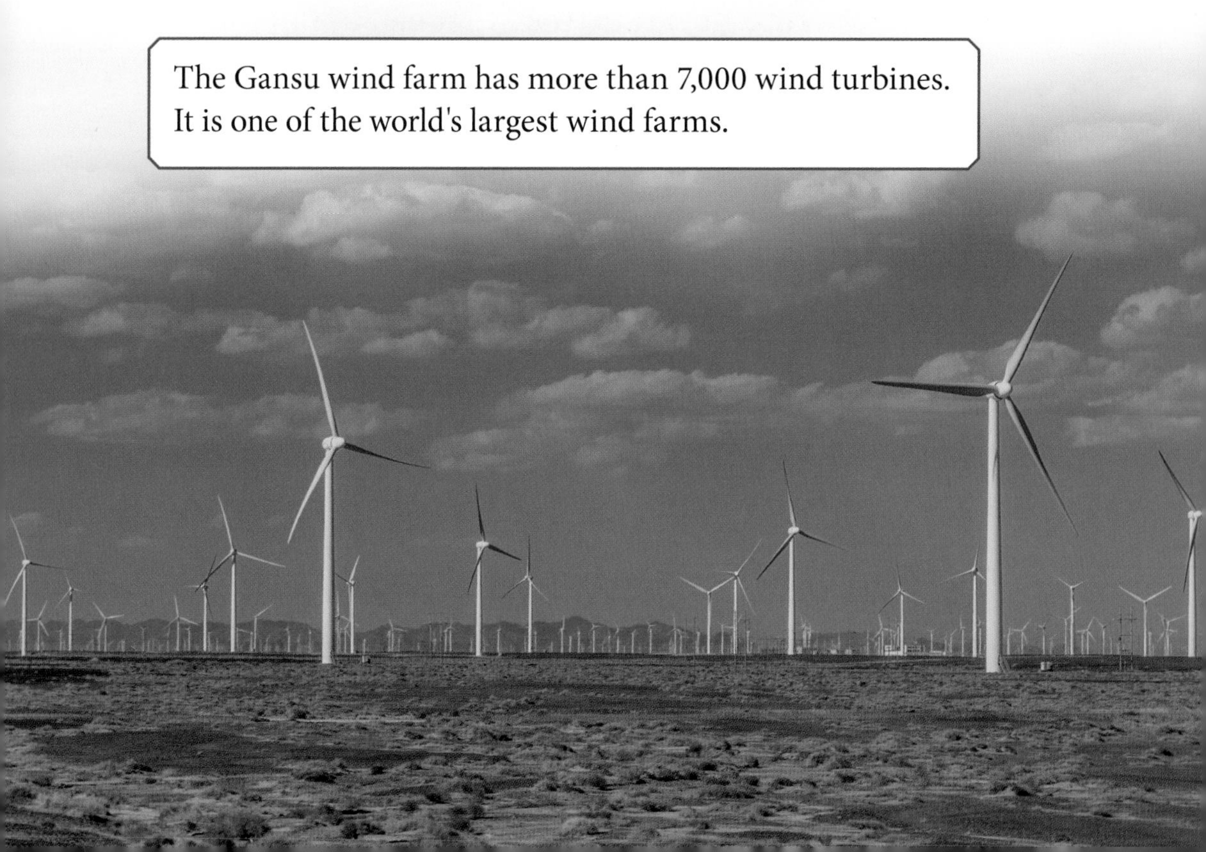

Wind farms can be found all over the world. They harness the wind's power to create electricity. Wind power saves us hours of backbreaking labor that people had to perform in the Middle Ages.

FACT

A land wind turbine in Germany soars to 584 feet (178 m) tall. That's taller than the Great Pyramid of Giza in Egypt!

Most medieval people spent their days growing, harvesting, or processing food. Grinding grain into flour took a long time. This job was usually done by women. To grind the grain, they first had to roll the wheat stalk between their hands. This caused the seeds to fall off. Then they used stones to grind the seeds into flour. This process could take hours. Then, women still had to make bread with the flour.

Medieval people used large, circular stones called millstones to grind grain.

A post mill called the Bonne Chiere windmill is located in Brugge, Belgium.

Post Mills

Sometime in the 1100s, windmills appeared in northern Europe. They were called post mills. A post mill was a wooden, box-shaped structure with blades attached. When the wind blew, it turned the blades. The spinning blades turned a crank inside the structure. If the wind changed directions, workers used a post under the mill to turn the structure toward the wind. The post mill needed to face the wind to work.

Water mills

Medieval workers had two sources of natural power—wind power and waterpower. Water mills were used before the Middle Ages. Flowing water from rivers and streams turned a large wooden wheel on the water mill. The wheel turned a shaft, which was attached to a millstone. The millstone ground the grain into flour. But water mills were expensive to build. Most medieval people couldn't afford them.

Northern Europe had cold winters. Rivers and streams froze during the cold months. Water mills sat empty and unused until the spring and summer. Medieval people in these areas turned to the windmill to make flour.

Fixed Tower Windmills

By the 1400s, fixed tower windmills emerged. These windmills didn't move. They were built out of stone or brick. The blades were attached to a wooden cap at the top of the tower. The cap could be rotated on a track. Workers turned the blades when the wind changed directions. Fixed tower windmills were sturdier than post mills. They could hold larger blades. This produced more power.

Lords and Mills

Only wealthy **lords** could afford to build water mills and windmills. **Peasants** had to pay a fee to grind their grains at a lord's mill. Peasants had to give some of their grain to the lord as well.

Tidal Mills, Fulling Mills, and Sawmills

During the 1000s, the tidal mill was introduced in Europe. A tidal mill used ocean tides for power. It was an ideal mill for those who did not have access to flowing water. This mill only worked when the ocean tides were high. High tides meant higher ocean levels at shore.

By the 1200s, fulling mills and sawmills were also in operation. A fulling mill made wool fabric. Sawmills cut wood for buildings, houses, and machines.

The Triphammer

A steel company in California installed one of the world's largest **hydraulic** power hammers in 2010. This machine weighs 2,650 tons and stands more than 60 feet (18 m) tall. The large metal hammer can drop 40,000 tons of force in a single blow. Workers use it to **forge** giant steel parts for aircraft and jet fighters.

Metal shops around the world use power hammers. Many are small enough to fit inside a garage. They are powerful enough to bend and shape metal easily. They can be run by motors or compressed air. Today's power hammers are based on the giant hammers that medieval workers used more than 500 years ago.

Power hammers are used to make items such as metal tools, car parts, and nails.

In the Early Middle Ages, metalworkers had to pound metal by hand. They slammed metal hammers onto anvils over and over again. Metalworking was exhausting.

Creative workers decided to try using water mills for more than just grinding grain. They built gears to power giant hammers, called triphammers. Triphammers were made of wood and iron. As the waterwheel turned, it raised the triphammer. Then the triphammer was dropped with a heavy, pounding force.

Beer making

The water-powered triphammer was used to make many products during medieval times. Beermakers may have been one of the first to use the new technology. Historians found the building plans for a **monastery** built in Switzerland around AD 820. The plans showed circles with hammer-like objects attached. A brewery was located next to the monastery. Historians believe people at the monastery used triphammers to crush barley into malt to make beer.

Workers in the Middle Ages beat heated iron by hand or with water-powered triphammers to make tools.

Manufacturing Armor

Mention the Middle Ages and most people think of a knight wearing a gleaming suit of armor. During medieval times, a knight's armor was made of iron or steel. It protected knights from swords and arrows during battle. But only skilled metalworkers called armorers could make these complex suits of armor.

To make a knight's armor, armorers needed iron. Miners dug rocks that contained iron ore. These rocks had to be crushed to reach the ore. Before triphammers, men had to smash the rocks apart by hand. Now the triphammer did the job for them. The rocks were heated to a very high temperature to separate the metal from the rock.

Armorers heated up iron to 2,700 degrees Fahrenheit (1,500 degrees Celsius). This heat turned the iron into steel. Triphammers pounded the steel into rough plates.

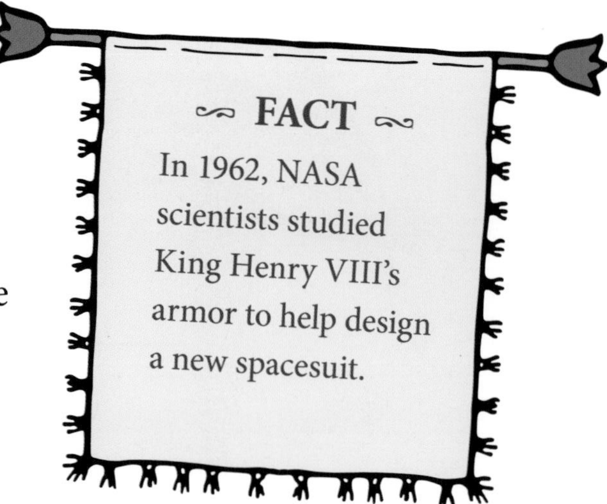

Once the plates had their shapes, the armorer would try to put the plates together. If everything fit, the armorer would smooth the plates by hand and assemble them.

Suit of Armor

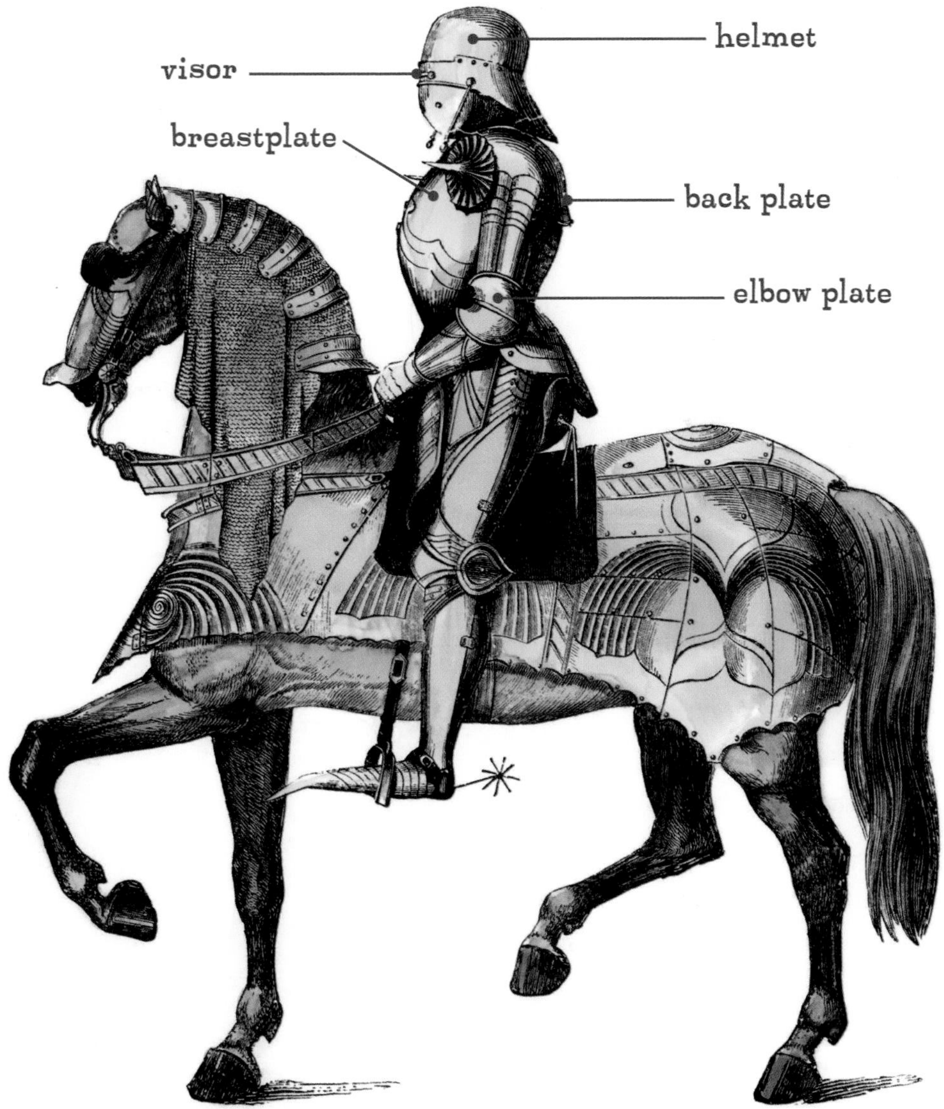

Making Cloth

Triphammers were also used to make woolen clothing. First, a sheep's wool was sheared off. Then the wool was cleaned, spun into yarn, and made into cloth. Medieval workers used triphammers to pound the woolen cloth. This caused the wool fibers in the cloth to stick together, making the cloth thicker and stronger.

Medieval workers used triphammers to make linen cloth as well. Flax has very stiff fibers. The triphammers pounded and softened them. Once the fibers were soft enough, they were spun into thread. The thread was woven into linen fabrics.

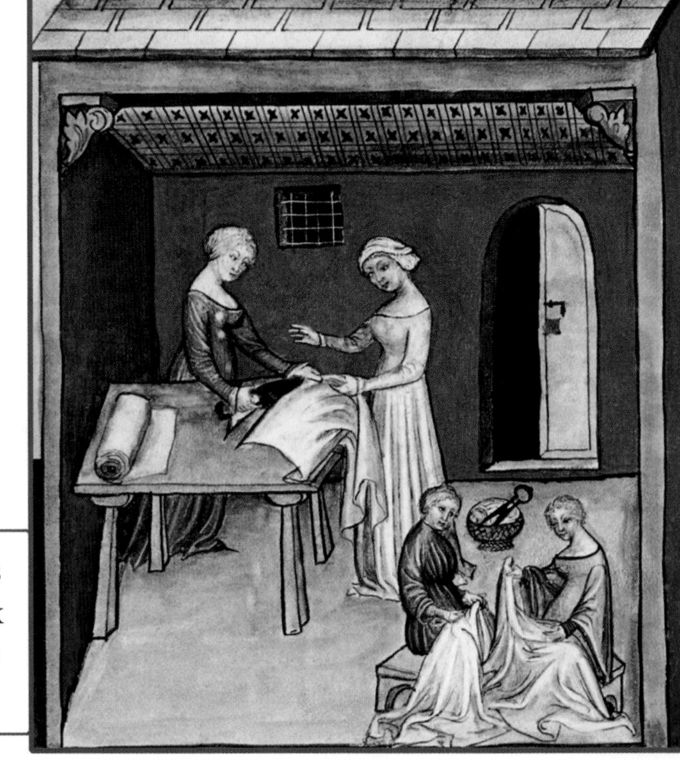

Medieval triphammers were used to crush flax plants quickly to make linen fabrics.

To make paper, medieval workers placed materials in a trough. Then they used hammers powered by water wheels to pound down the material.

Papermaking

In the mid-1100s, triphammers were used in Spain and Italy to make paper. This paper was made with fabric and other organic fibers. The triphammer beat these materials together into a pulp. The pulp was then pressed into thin sheets and left to dry. This technology spread to France in the 1300s and to England in the 1400s. The triphammer made it easier for workers to make paper. Paper became less expensive. For the first time, many people could afford it.

The Spinning Wheel

Have you ever wondered how your clothes are made? Clothing starts with thread or yarn that is woven into cloth. Today, most thread and yarn is made in factories. Cotton is one of the most-used fabrics in the world. To make cotton into thread, a machine cleans the cotton fibers. Then the fibers pass into a dryer that blows them into a web. The web is twisted into thick coils. The coils are stretched and combed until they are very thin. Finally, the thin strings are spun into thread on a ring-spinning machine.

In the Early Middle Ages, thread and yarn weren't made by machines. Women spun yarn by hand. A mass of loose fibers was wrapped around a large stick called a distaff.

Women pulled and twisted these fibers together with their fingers to make yarn. They wound the yarn around wooden shafts called spindles. Spinning yarn was a slow process. Women often had to stand for hours while they worked.

Hundreds of rolls of cotton thread can be spun in only a few minutes in factories.

Spinning Wheel in Medieval Europe

The spinning wheel twists fibers into thread and yarn. Historians can't agree on when and where the spinning wheel was first used. It may have been invented in India around AD 500 or in China around the year 1000. The technology arrived in Europe in the 1200s or 1300s.

The spinning wheel sped up the production of yarn in the Middle Ages. The first spinning wheels in Europe had a wheel attached to the spindle by a **pulley**. Women would turn the wheel by hand to spin the spindle. The spinning motion of the wheel slowly pulled and twisted the fibers from the distaff onto the spindle. It sped up production and made the yarn pieces look the same.

To spin thread, spinners held the distaff in one hand while slowly turning the spinning wheel with the other.

By the 1500s, a new version of the spinning wheel freed up workers' hands. They could work even faster. The spinning wheel could be operated by a foot pedal, called a **treadle**. The distaff was fixed in place, so the worker no longer had to hold it.

Sleeping Beauty

One of the earliest versions of the fairy tale "Sleeping Beauty" was written in the Middle Ages. In the story, a princess falls into a deep sleep while spinning yarn. Nothing can wake her, and she is placed in a high tower. In later versions, she pricks her finger on a spinning wheel before falling asleep.

The Horizontal Loom

Spinning yarn and thread is only the first step to make fabric. Today's factories weave thread on looms to make fabric. Computer-controlled looms shoot the thread into the loom using puffs of air. The loom weaves some threads horizontally and others vertically, like a basket. The fastest looms can shoot more than 2,000 horizontal threads per minute. Other types of looms use thousands of small needles to knit the threads together with tiny loops.

Today's weaving looms can create thousands of different fabric patterns and textures.

Weavers using vertical frame looms often tied stones to the bottom of yarn to keep it tight.

In the Early Middle Ages, women wove cloth by hand using **vertical** frame looms. First, yarn was hung at the top of a wood frame. To keep the pieces tight, weavers tied weights to the bottom of the yarn. Then, weavers wove more yarn sideways through the vertical pieces. Standing in front of the loom to weave was difficult work. And the size of the cloth they could make was limited to the size of the loom.

FACT

Looms were used long before the Middle Ages. They were used in China at least 4,000 years ago.

The Horizontal Loom

As the Middle Ages continued, looms changed. One of the first horizontal looms in medieval Europe was from the 1000s. The loom was laid flat. Weavers could sit at these machines. The horizontal looms were much larger than vertical looms, allowing larger pieces of fabric to be made. Weavers spent less energy making more fabric at a faster rate.

Weavers operated horizontal looms with foot pedals.

Medieval Clothing

Most medieval people wore simple clothing made of wool or linen. Men wore undershirts and tunics. Tunics were T-shaped, making them easy to move in. Women wore long dresses down to their ankles. The dresses were fitted around the upper body. The sleeves flared out. Women were expected to cover their heads in public. Most wore veils attached to headbands. The veil covered the sides and back of a woman's head.

The Fabric Industry in the Middle Ages

As the Middle Ages progressed, making fabric became more important. The horizontal loom helped the fabric industry grow. Horizontal looms were expensive to build and maintain. Most weavers could not afford to have one in their homes. Men began working in factories to weave fabric on horizontal looms. Women also worked in this industry, but men usually got the better-paying jobs.

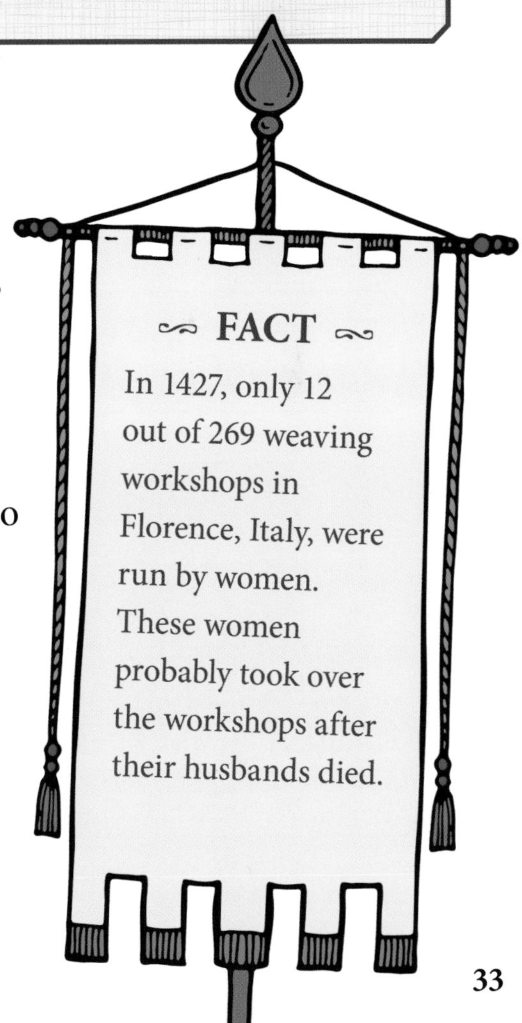

The Suction Pump

In South Africa, the Mponeng gold mine runs deep below the earth's surface. It's one of the deepest mines on the planet. Miners travel more than 2 miles (3.2 kilometers) underground each day. The trip down takes more than an hour! Giant fans bring fresh air to workers below. Deep underground, the earth gets hot. It can reach 140 °F (60 °C). Pumps push icy sludge into the mine to bring the temperature down.

The Mponeng gold mine is the deepest gold mine in the world.

Like all underground mines, Mponeng must keep out extra water. Flooded mines were dangerous for miners. Below a certain level called the water table, soil and rock are soaked with water. Drilling below the water table means water will seep into a mine. Miners use suction pumps to remove the water. Motors run these heavy-duty pumps. Some pumping systems use pits. Water seeps into the pits. Then the pumps bring the water out of the mine.

Even with modern technology, mining is dangerous work. In the Middle Ages, it was even more dangerous for miners. Medieval miners ran into problems with wet mines as well. They had to abandon flooded mines. Miners came up with different ways to keep the mines dry.

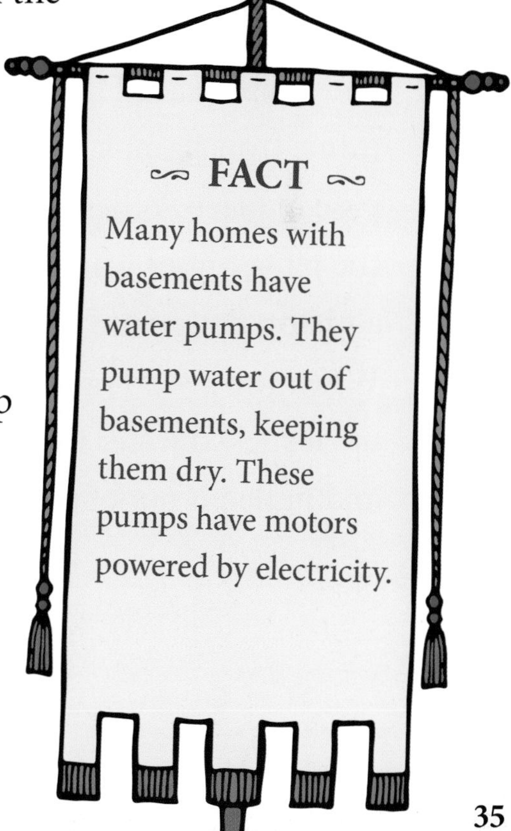

FACT

Many homes with basements have water pumps. They pump water out of basements, keeping them dry. These pumps have motors powered by electricity.

Valuable Mines

Mining for metals and minerals was an important industry in medieval times. Medieval money was made from silver or gold. Mines that produced these metals were valuable. Workers also used metal to make armor, tools, and other items. Miners in the Late Middle Ages started digging deeper to find metals.

Suction Pumps

The suction pump was developed during the Middle Ages in the 1400s and 1500s. This pump had a pipe placed in a pit in the mine. Iron clamps kept the pipe in place. When water filled the pit, a miner would push a **piston** down into the pipe. When the piston raised back up, it sucked water into the pipe and pulled it out of the mine.

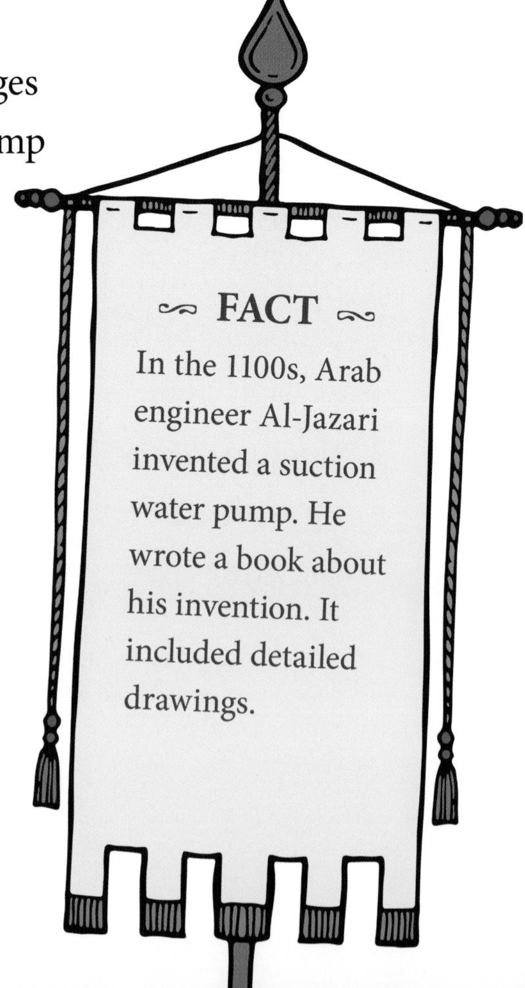

FACT

In the 1100s, Arab engineer Al-Jazari invented a suction water pump. He wrote a book about his invention. It included detailed drawings.

More powerful, complex pumps were developed toward the end of the Middle Ages. These pumps had more than one pit and pipe. Some were powered by water wheels.

Medieval miners removed water from a mine using water wheels and suction pumps.

The Wheelbarrow

The wheelbarrow is a simple yet powerful tool that moves loads of materials quickly and easily. People use them in yard projects and at construction sites. Most people use standard wheelbarrows. You pick up the handles and push it forward on one wheel. Motorized wheelbarrows take this to another level. They can haul 1,000 pounds (450 kilograms) or more in a single load! A motor pushes the wheelbarrow forward. Some can even dump with the press of a button. These machines save time and energy.

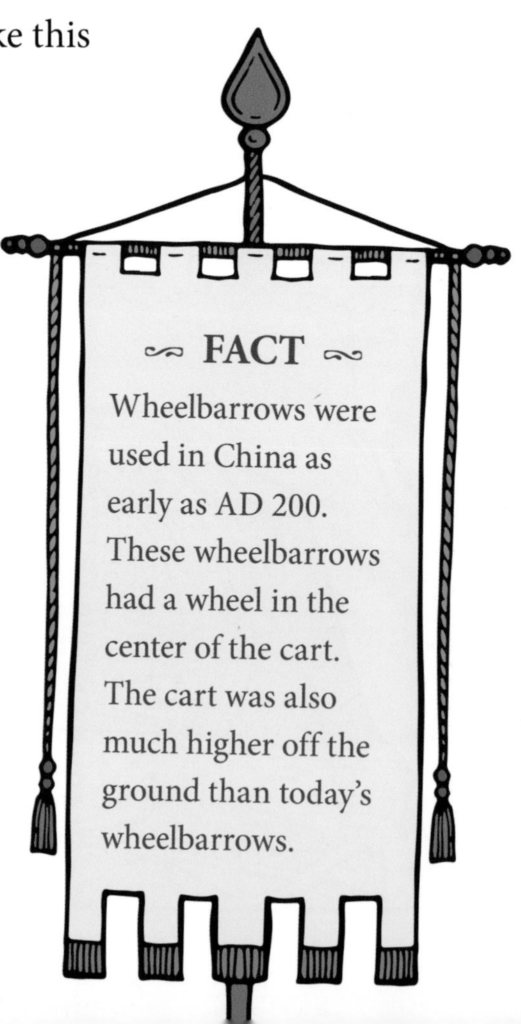

FACT

Wheelbarrows were used in China as early as AD 200. These wheelbarrows had a wheel in the center of the cart. The cart was also much higher off the ground than today's wheelbarrows.

Medieval workers used wheelbarrows in mines and while making buildings, castles, and churches.

For hundreds of years, medieval workers moved heavy loads by hand or with handbarrows. A handbarrow looked like a wheelbarrow without the wheel. Two workers had to lift up the load together.

By the early 1200s, medieval workers started using wheelbarrows. This small wooden cart had a wheel and an **axle** at the front. It made moving rocks and supplies much easier.

The Printing Press

Imagine all the printed words, photos, and illustrations you see during the day. How do you think they are printed? The KBA Rapida 205 is one of the world's largest printing presses. It can print 9,000 sheets of paper in one hour. This printer can handle sheets as big as 6.75 by 5 feet (2 by 1.5 m)! Special lights dry the ink almost instantly. Like many modern printing presses, the Rapida 205 uses offset printing. In offset printing, a rubber cylinder is rolled over the paper, leaving behind images or words.

In the Middle Ages, printing was rare and expensive. Most books had to be written by hand on pieces of **parchment**. Parchment was made from sheep, goat, or calf skins. Many medieval books contained painted illustrations, making them even more expensive. Owning even one book was too costly for most medieval people. Castles with private libraries were famous.

Printing in Asia

During the Middle Ages, Asia was ahead of Europe when it came to printed materials. The oldest known printed book was created in China in AD 868. Called *The Diamond Sutra,* this book was printed using wooden blocks.

Moveable type came next. In moveable type printing, letters are printed on blocks that can be reused over and over. Inventor Bi Sheng created this method in China around the year 1000. He used clay blocks instead of wood. Printed books became more common in China by the 1200s.

The Printing Press in Europe

In 1440, a German inventor named Johannes Gutenberg moved to France. He began experimenting with a moveable type printing press. This machine pressed ink onto paper. Gutenberg used metal blocks instead of wooden or clay blocks. Each letter of the alphabet had its own block. Gutenberg also invented a special ink that stuck to the metal blocks.

In 1450, Gutenberg returned to Germany and opened a print shop. His press could print about 200 sheets of paper per hour. Gutenberg printed pamphlets and calendars.

Soon, the printing press spread from Germany to the rest of Europe. Books became cheaper and easier to print. More people could afford them. Ideas and information spread as more people learned to read. Gutenberg's printing press helped usher in the age of modern printing.

The Importance of Medieval Manufacturing

The Middle Ages are often described as a period with very little cultural or industrial progress. But history shows that many major technological advances were made by medieval people. Their inventions improved manufacturing practices we still use today.

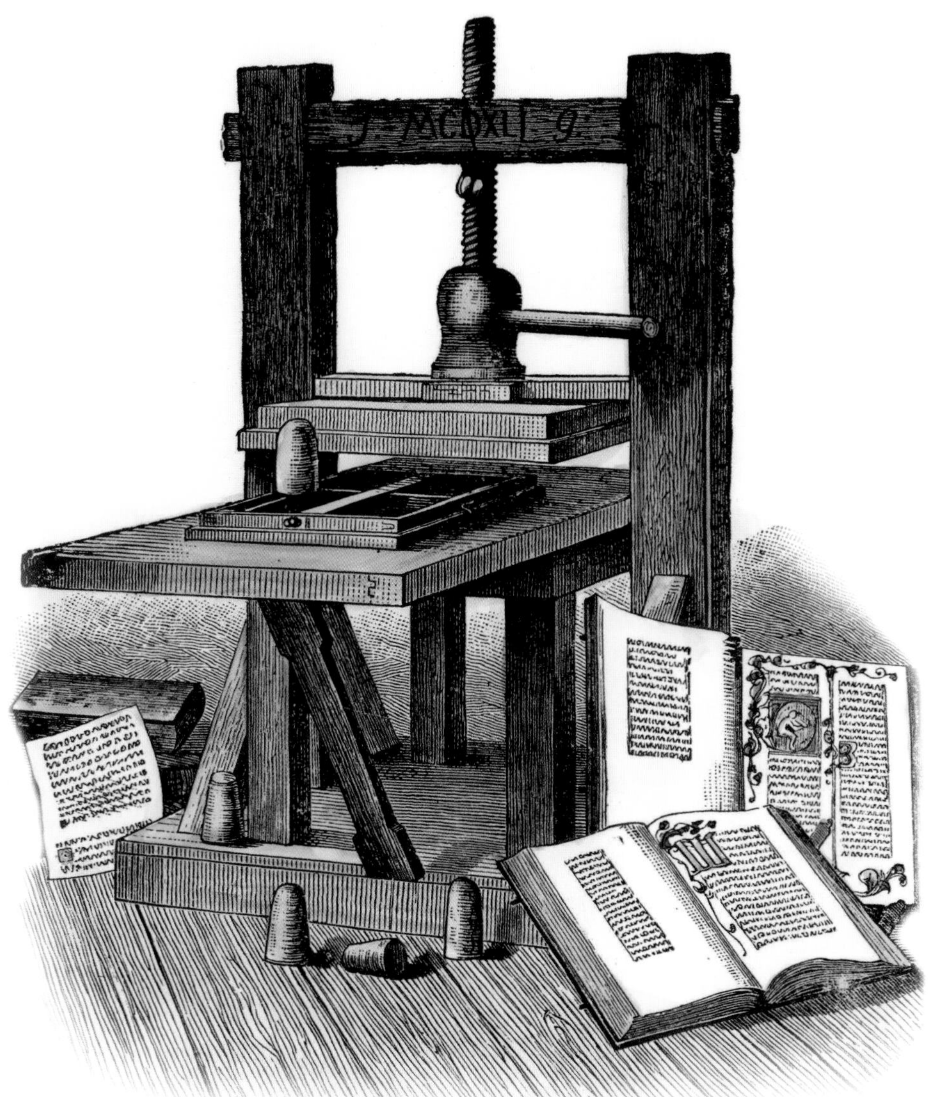

Timeline of Technology

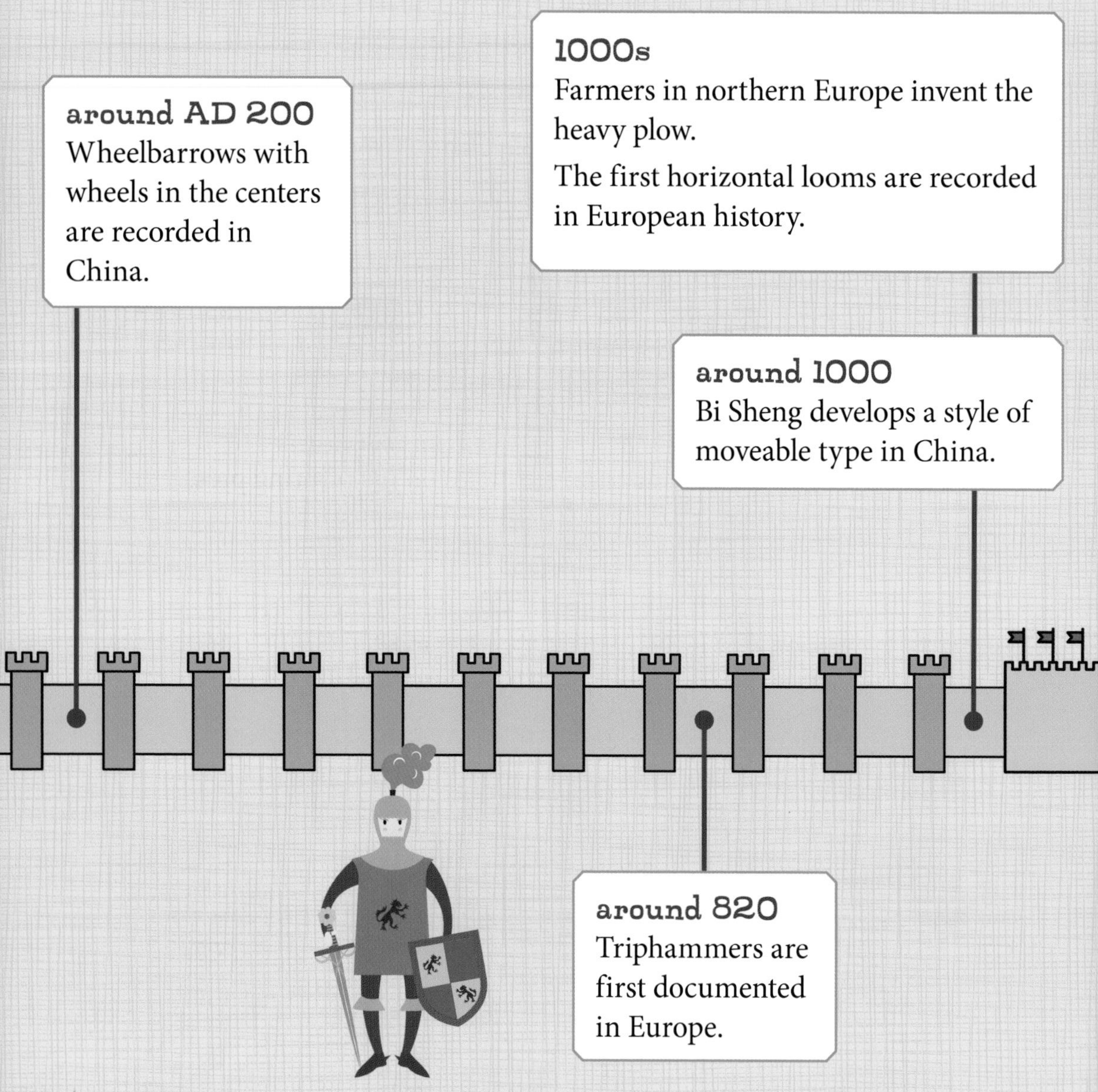

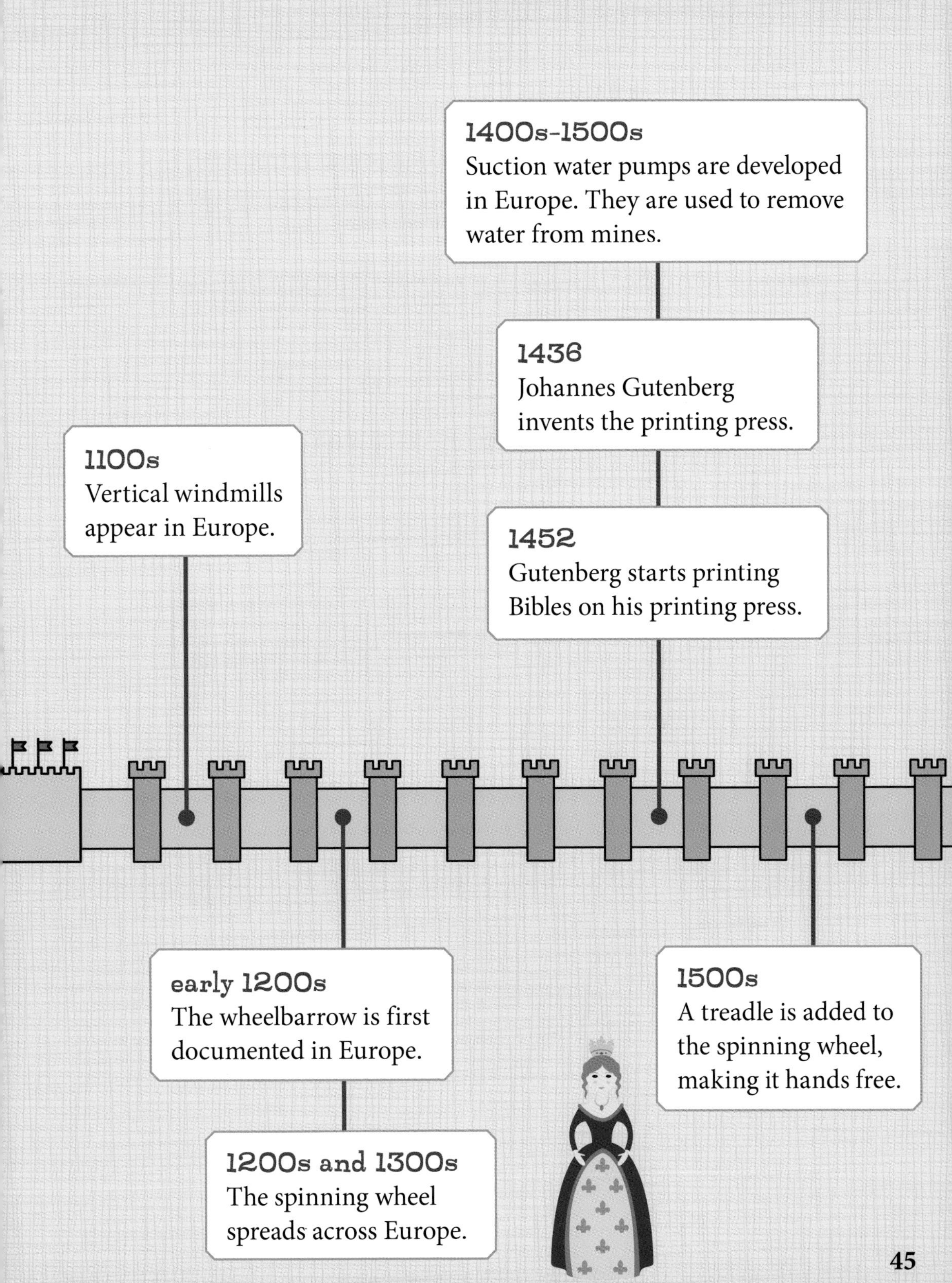
1400s–1500s
Suction water pumps are developed in Europe. They are used to remove water from mines.
1436
Johannes Gutenberg invents the printing press.
1100s
Vertical windmills appear in Europe.
1452
Gutenberg starts printing Bibles on his printing press.
early 1200s
The wheelbarrow is first documented in Europe.
1500s
A treadle is added to the spinning wheel, making it hands free.
1200s and 1300s
The spinning wheel spreads across Europe.

Glossary

axle (AK-suhl)—a bar in the center of a wheel

flax (FLAKS)—plant that can be used to make linen for fabric

forge (FORJ)—form something from metal using heat

generator (JEN-uh-ray-tur)—a machine that makes electricity by turning a magnet inside a coil of wire

hydraulic (hye-DRAW-lik)—having to do with a system powered by fluid forced through pipes or chambers

lord (LORD)—a person of high rank who has great power

manufacturing (man-yuh-FAK-chur-ing)—the process of making goods, often in factories

monastery (MAH-nuh-ster-ee)—a group of buildings where monks live and work

peasant (PEZ-uhnt)—a small-scale farmer who grows his or her own food

piston (PIS-tuhn)—a part inside a machine that moves up and down, expanding and compressing fluid or air

pulley (PUL-ee)—a grooved wheel turned by a rope, belt, or chain that often moves heavy objects

treadle (TREH-duhl)—a lever pumped by a person's foot to drive a machine

turbine (TUR-bine)—a machine with blades that can be turned by wind

Read More

Lassieur, Allison. *Medieval Knight Science: Armor, Weapons, and Siege Warfare*. North Mankato, MN: Capstone Press, 2017.

Roesser, Marie. *The Middle Ages*. New York: Gareth Stevens Publishing, 2020.

Stokes, Jonathan W. *The Thrifty Guide to Medieval Times: A Handbook for Time Travelers*. New York: Penguin Group, 2019.

Internet Sites

History for Kids: The Amazing Middle Ages.
https://www.historyforkids.net/middle-ages.html

DK Find Out: Castles.
https://www.dkfindout.com/us/history/castles/

Select Bibliography

Langdon, John. *Mills in the Medieval Economy*. Oxford: Oxford University Press, 2004.

Newman, Paul B. *Daily Life in the Middle Ages*. London: McFarland and Co., 2001.

Riddle, John M. *A History of the Middle Ages 300-1500*. Lanham, Maryland: Rowman & Littlefield, 2016.

Index